Goodnight, My Love!
ราตรีสวัสดิ์ ลูกรัก

Shelley Admont
Illustrated by Samir Boumsik

www.kidkiddos.com
Copyright©2016 by S.A. Publishing ©2017 KidKiddos Books Ltd.
support@kidkiddos.com

All rights reserved. No part of this book may be reproduced in any form or by any electronic or mechanical means, including information storage and retrieval systems, without written permission from the publisher or author, except in the case of a reviewer, who may quote brief passages embodied in critical articles or in a review. First edition

Translated from English by Lalida Puengklai
แปลจากภาษาอังกฤษโดย ลลิดา พึ่งคล้าย

Library and Archives Canada Cataloguing in Publication
Goodnight, My Love! (English Thai Bilingual Edition)/ Shelley Admont
ISBN: 978-1-5259-5802-1 paperback
ISBN: 978-1-5259-5803-8 hardcover
ISBN: 978-1-5259-5801-4 eBook

Please note that the Thai and English versions of the story have been written to be as close as possible. However, in some cases they differ in order to accommodate nuances and fluidity of each language.

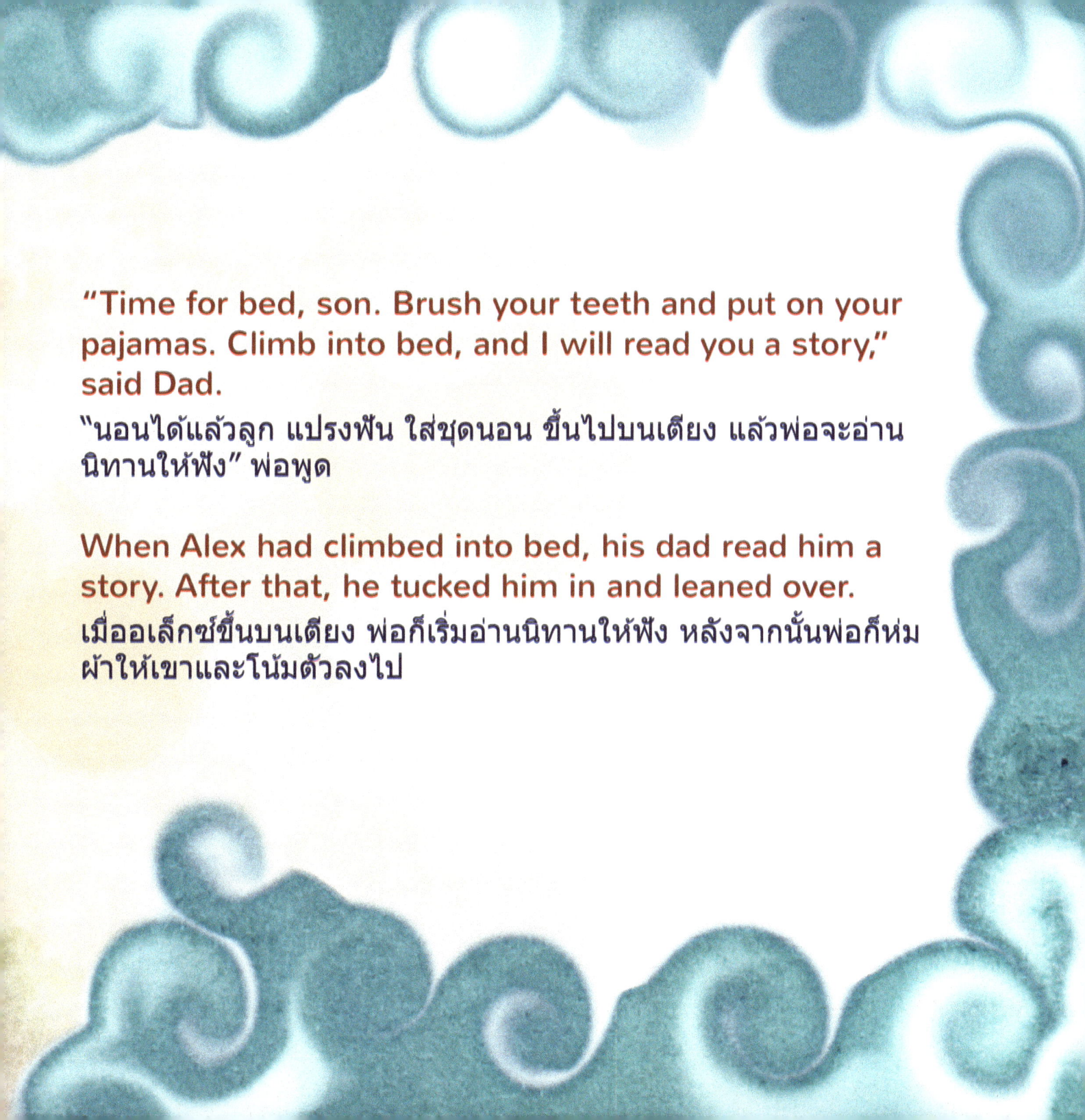

"Time for bed, son. Brush your teeth and put on your pajamas. Climb into bed, and I will read you a story," said Dad.

"นอนได้แล้วลูก แปรงฟัน ใส่ชุดนอน ขึ้นไปบนเตียง แล้วพ่อจะอ่านนิทานให้ฟัง" พ่อพูด

When Alex had climbed into bed, his dad read him a story. After that, he tucked him in and leaned over.

เมื่ออเล็กซ์ขึ้นบนเตียง พ่อก็เริ่มอ่านนิทานให้ฟัง หลังจากนั้นพ่อก็ห่มผ้าให้เขาและโน้มตัวลงไป

"Goodnight, son. Goodnight, dear. I love you," he said.
"ราตรีสวัสดิ์นะลูกชาย ราตรีสวัสดิ์ลูกรัก พ่อรักลูกนะ" พ่อพูด

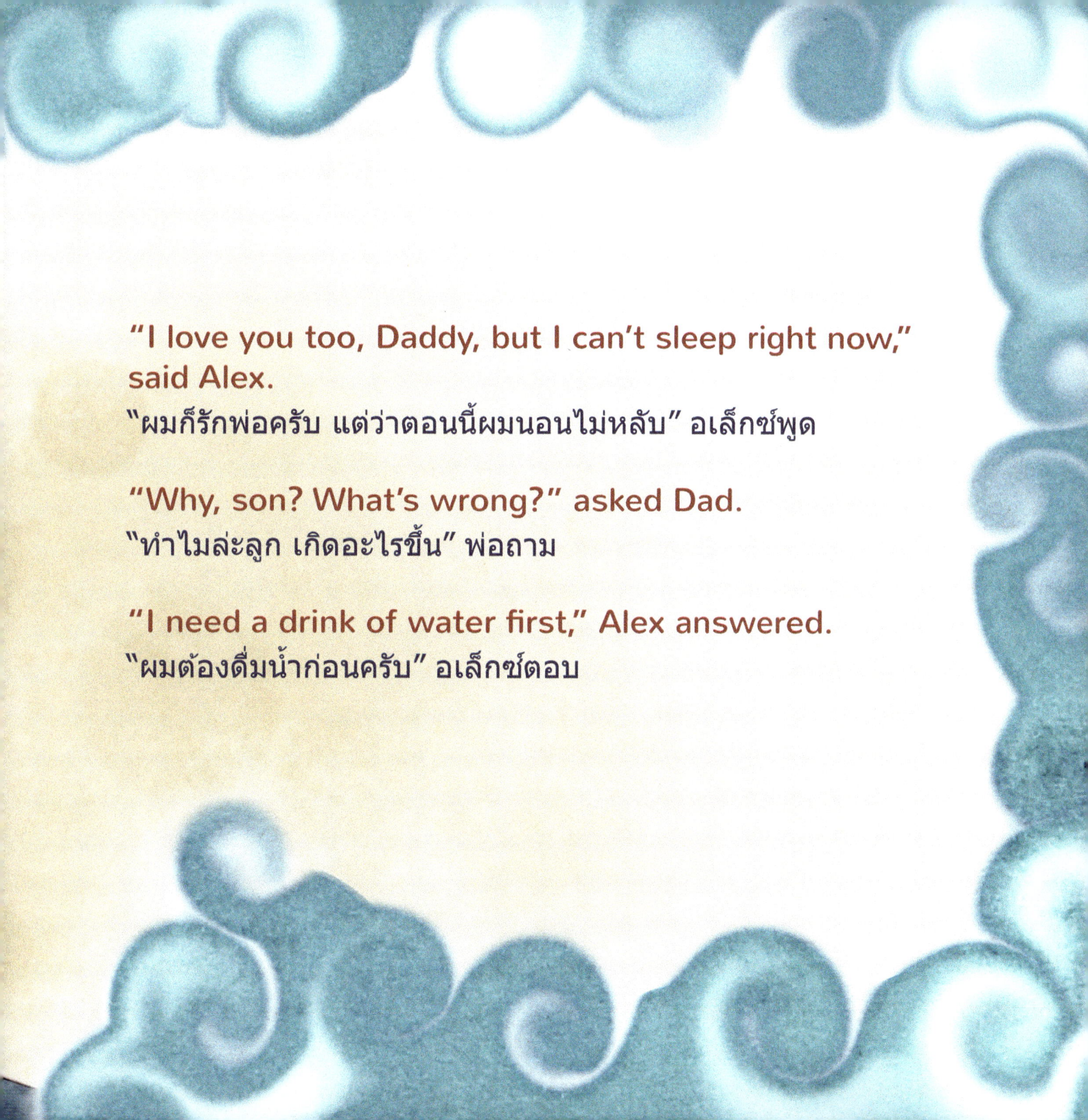

"I love you too, Daddy, but I can't sleep right now," said Alex.
"ผมก็รักพ่อครับ แต่ว่าตอนนี้ผมนอนไม่หลับ" อเล็กซ์พูด

"Why, son? What's wrong?" asked Dad.
"ทำไมล่ะลูก เกิดอะไรขึ้น" พ่อถาม

"I need a drink of water first," Alex answered.
"ผมต้องดื่มน้ำก่อนครับ" อเล็กซ์ตอบ

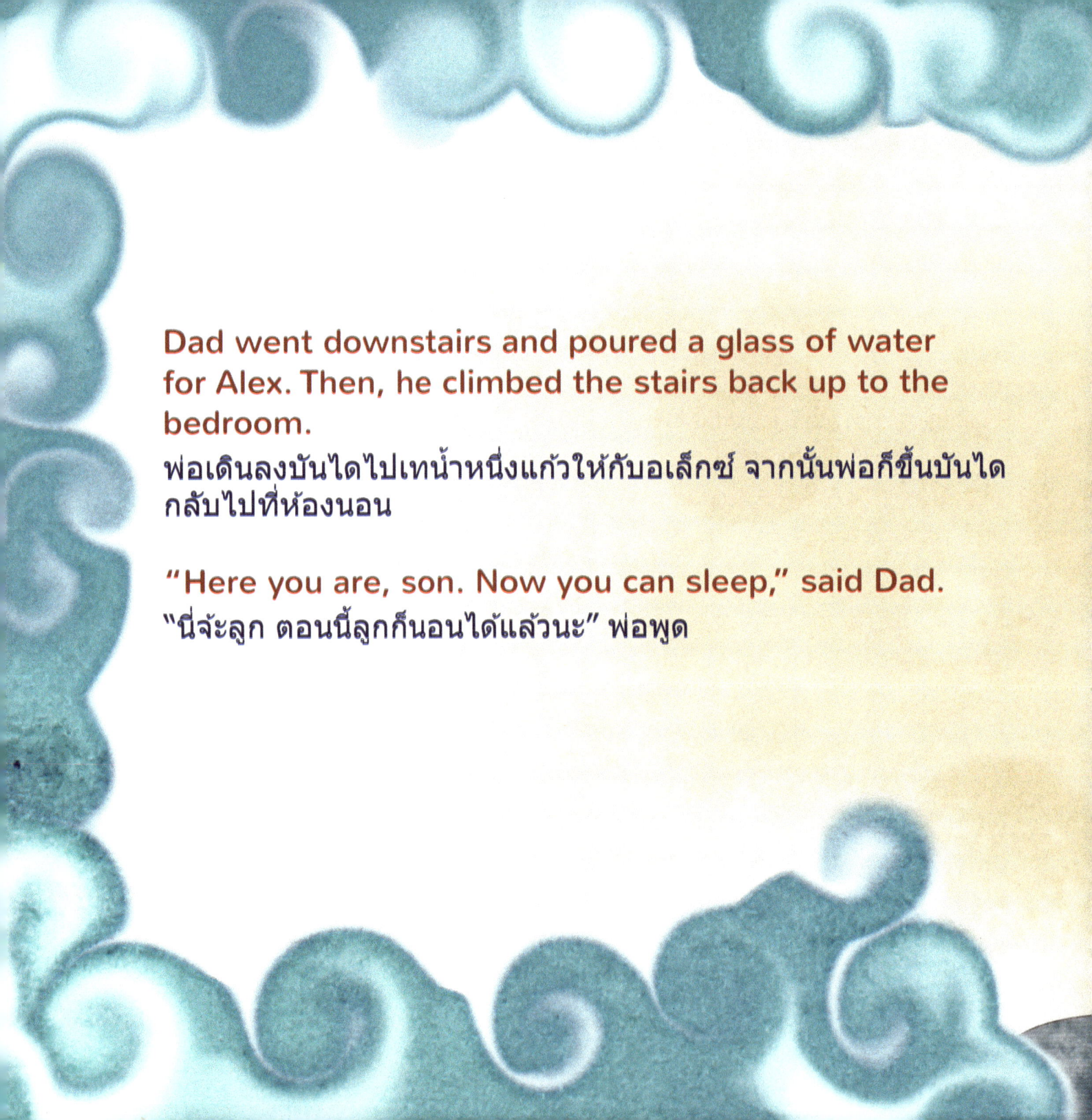

Dad went downstairs and poured a glass of water for Alex. Then, he climbed the stairs back up to the bedroom.
พ่อเดินลงบันไดไปเทน้ำหนึ่งแก้วให้กับอเล็กซ์ จากนั้นพ่อก็ขึ้นบันไดกลับไปที่ห้องนอน

"Here you are, son. Now you can sleep," said Dad.
"นี่จ้ะลูก ตอนนี้ลูกก็นอนได้แล้วนะ" พ่อพูด

Alex drank the glass of water and lay back down. His dad tucked him in and leaned over.
อเล็กซ์ดื่มน้ำแก้วนั้นและล้มตัวลงนอน พ่อห่มผ้าให้เขาและโน้มตัวลงไป

"Goodnight, son. Goodnight, dear. I love you," he said.
"ราตรีสวัสดิ์นะลูกชาย ราตรีสวัสดิ์ลูกรัก พ่อรักลูกนะ" พ่อพูด

"I love you too, Daddy, but I can't sleep right now."
"ผมก็รักพ่อครับ แต่ว่าตอนนี้ผมนอนไม่หลับ"

"Why, son? What's wrong?" asked Dad.
"ทำไมล่ะลูก เกิดอะไรขึ้น" พ่อถาม

"I need my teddy bear," answered Alex.
"ผมอยากได้ตุ๊กตาหมีของผมครับ" อเล็กซ์ตอบ

Dad walked across the room and picked up a blue teddy bear.
พ่อเดินไปที่อีกฝั่งของห้องและหยิบตุ๊กตาหมีสีน้ำเงินขึ้นมา

He brought it back and gave it to Alex.
พ่อถือตุ๊กตาตัวนั้นกลับมาและยื่นให้อเล็กซ์

"Not this one, Daddy. I need the gray teddy bear," said Alex.

"ไม่ใช่อันนี้ครับพ่อ ผมอยากได้ตุ๊กตาหมีสีเทา" อเล็กซ์พูด

Dad laughed. He went downstairs to get a gray teddy bear from the couch. Then, he climbed the stairs back up to his son's room again.

พ่อหัวเราะ เขาเดินลงบันไดไปหยิบตุ๊กตาสีเทาจากโซฟา จากนั้นเขาเดินขึ้นบันไดกลับไปยังห้องของลูกชายอีกครั้ง

"Here is your teddy bear. Now you can sleep," said Dad.
"นี่จ้ะ ตุ๊กตาหมีของลูก ตอนนี้ลูกก็ไปนอนได้แล้วนะ" พ่อพูด

"Thank you, Daddy!" said Alex.
"ขอบคุณครับพ่อ" อเล็กซ์พูด

Dad tucked in his son and the teddy bear and leaned over.
พ่อห่มผ้าให้กับลูกชายและตุ๊กตาหมี และโน้มตัวลงไป

"Goodnight, son. Goodnight, dear. I love you," he said.
"ราตรีสวัสดิ์นะลูกชาย ราตรีสวัสดิ์ลูกรัก พ่อรักลูกนะ" พ่อพูด

"I love you too, Daddy, but I still can't sleep yet," said Alex again.
"ผมก็รักพ่อครับ แต่ว่าตอนนี้ผมนอนไม่หลับ" อเล็กซ์พูดอีก

"Why, son? What's wrong?" asked Dad.
"ทำไมล่ะลูก เกิดอะไรขึ้น"

"Well, I don't know what to dream about," answered Alex.
"คือผมไม่รู้ว่าผมจะฝันเรื่องอะไรครับพ่อ" อเล็กซ์ตอบ

"Hmmm, that's very important, isn't it?" said Dad. Alex nodded.
"อืม นั่นเป็นเรื่องที่สำคัญมากเลยสินะ" พ่อพูด อเล็กซ์พยักหน้า

"Then, why don't we plan your dream together?" asked Dad.
"ถ้าอย่างนั้น ทำไมเราไม่มาวางแผนกันว่าเราจะฝันเรื่อง อะไรกันดี" พ่อถาม

"That's a good idea, Daddy!"
"เป็นความคิดที่ดีเลยครับพ่อ!"

"If you could be anything at all, Alex, what would you be?"
"ถ้าลูกเป็นอะไรก็ได้ อเล็กซ์ ลูกอยากจะเป็นอะไร"

"I'd be a bird and float on the breeze," answered Alex.
"ผมจะเป็นนกแล้วก็บินไปบนอากาศครับ" อเล็กซ์ตอบ

"What a beautiful dream, son!" said Dad.
"เป็นฝันที่สวยงามมากเลยลูก" พ่อพูด

"But, what will happen next?" asked Alex.
"แต่ว่า หลังจากนั้นจะเกิดอะไรขึ้นล่ะครับ" อเล็กซ์ถาม

"First, you and I will soar through the soft, fluffy clouds. The sun will warm our feathers," said Dad.
"เริ่มแรกลูกกับพ่อจะบินทะยานขึ้นไปบนก้อนเมฆนุ่ม ๆ แสงอาทิตย์จะทำให้ขนของเราอบอุ่น" พ่อพูด

"The sunrise is beautiful, Daddy!" said Alex. Dad nodded.
"พระอาทิตย์ขึ้นสวยมากเลยครับพ่อ!" อเล็กซ์พูด พ่อพยักหน้า

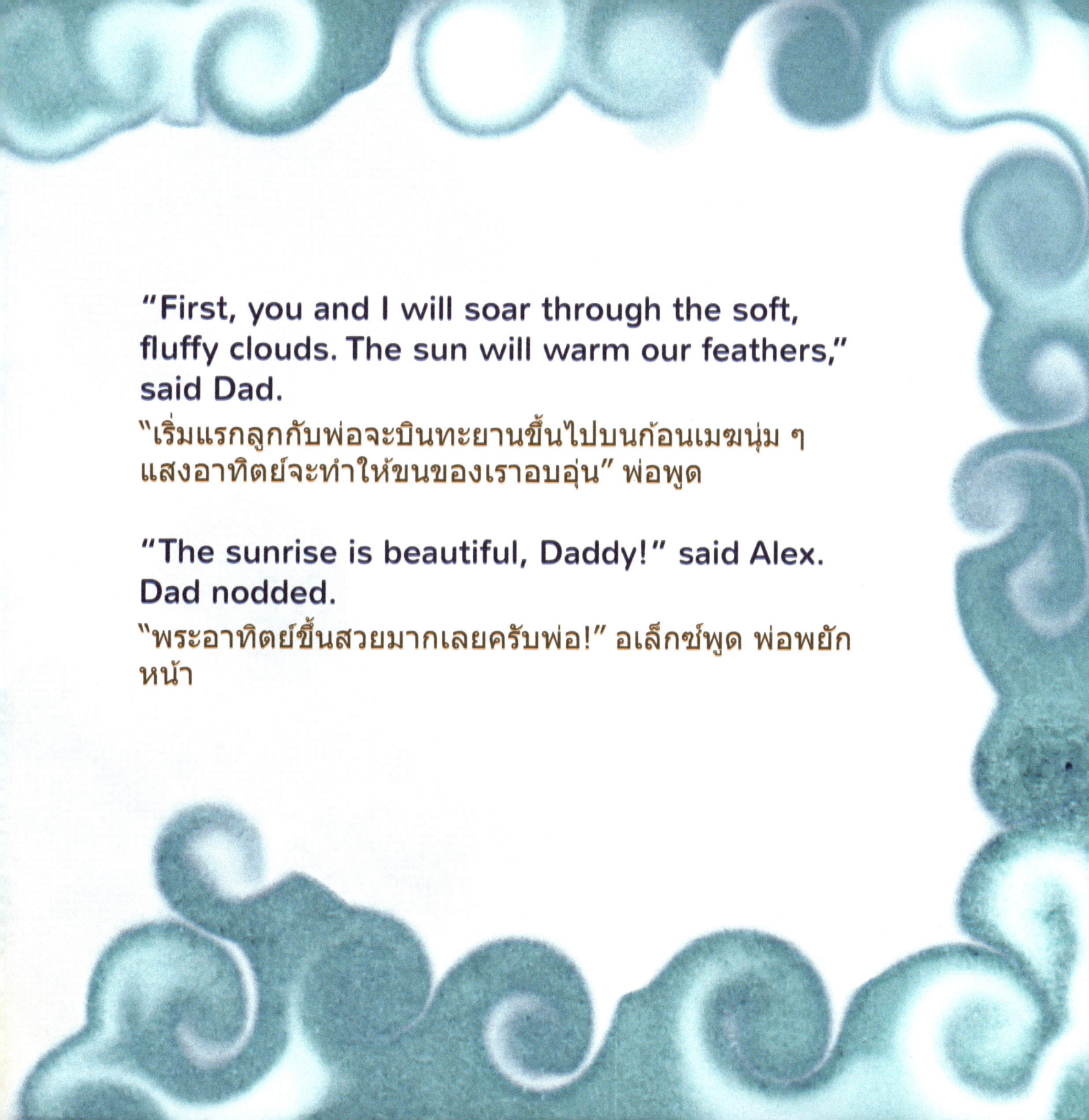

"Next, we will glide over the cool, gray mountains and past the quiet forest," said Dad.
"จากนั้นเราก็จะบินขึ้นเหนือภูเขาที่อากาศเย็นสบายและบินผ่านป่าอันเงียบสงบ" พ่อพูด

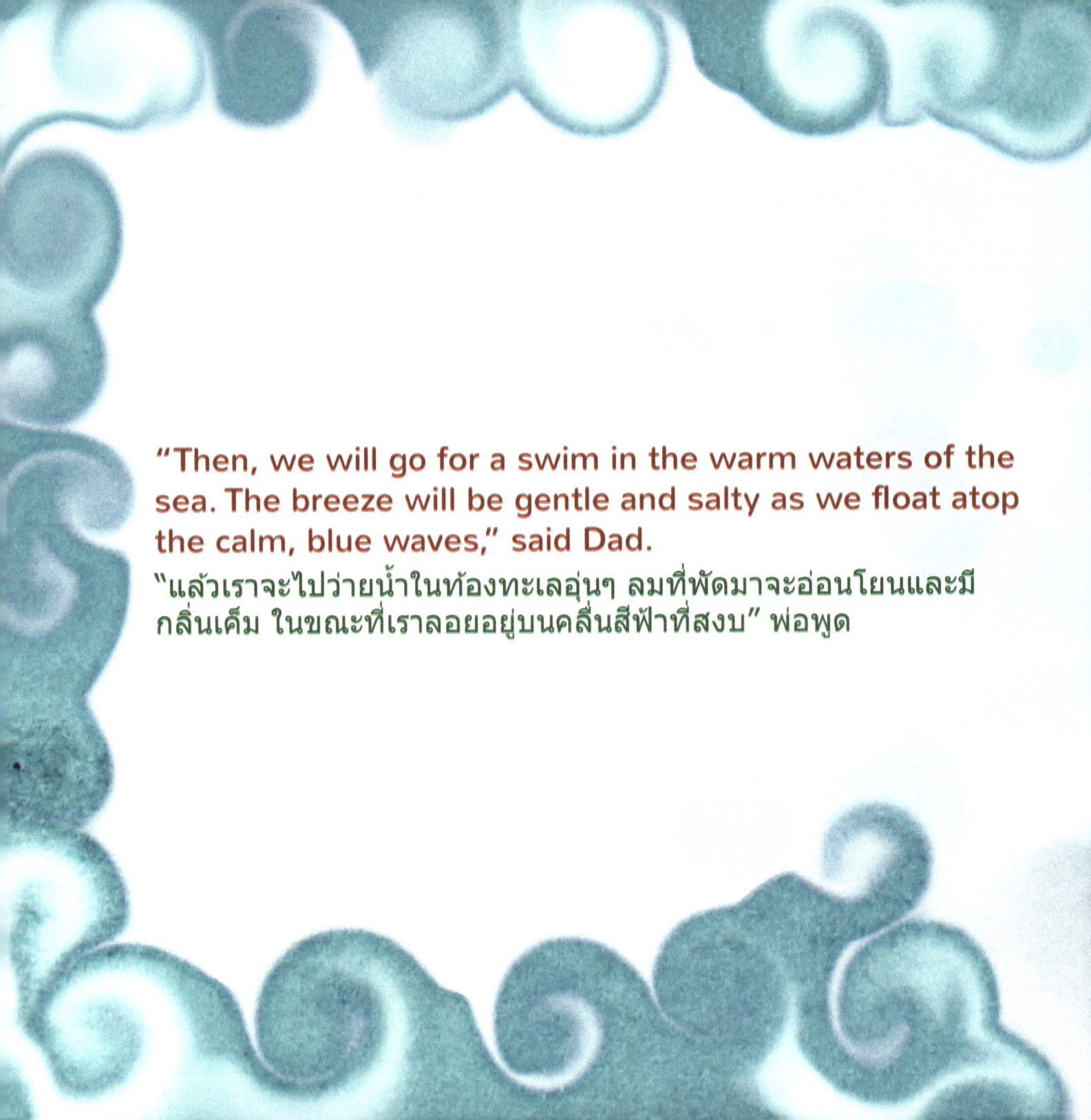

"Then, we will go for a swim in the warm waters of the sea. The breeze will be gentle and salty as we float atop the calm, blue waves," said Dad.

"แล้วเราจะไปว่ายน้ำในท้องทะเลอุ่นๆ ลมที่พัดมาจะอ่อนโยนและมีกลิ่นเค็ม ในขณะที่เราลอยอยู่บนคลื่นสีฟ้าที่สงบ" พ่อพูด

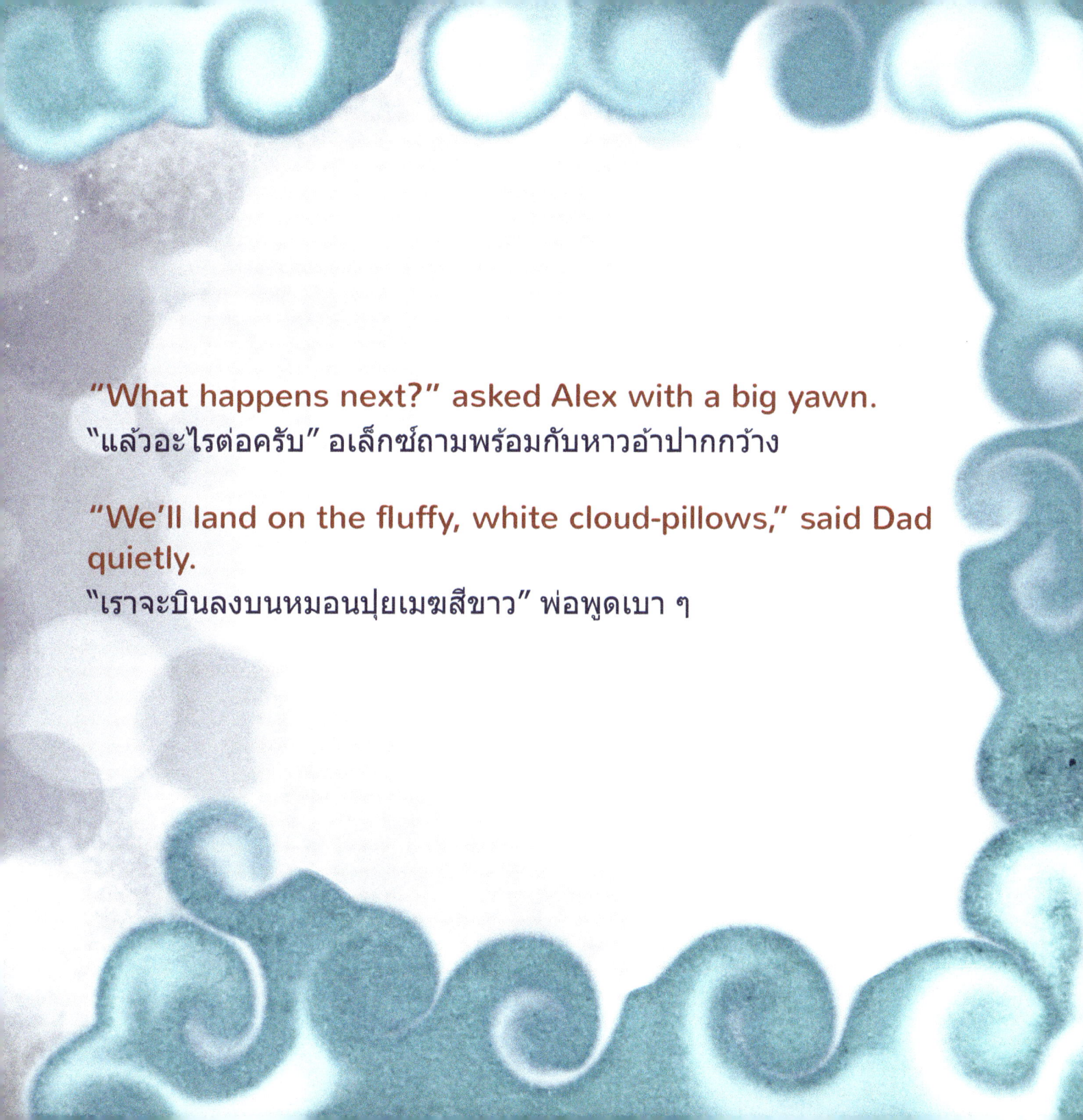

"What happens next?" asked Alex with a big yawn.
"แล้วอะไรต่อครับ" อเล็กซ์ถามพร้อมกับหาวอ้าปากกว้าง

"We'll land on the fluffy, white cloud-pillows," said Dad quietly.
"เราจะบินลงบนหมอนปุยเมฆสีขาว" พ่อพูดเบา ๆ

Dad looked at Alex sleeping and leaned over.
พ่อมองอเล็กซ์และโน้มตัวเข้าไป

"Goodnight, son. Goodnight, dear. I love you," said Dad. Then, he gave his son a kiss on his forehead.
"ราตรีสวัสดิ์นะลูกชาย ราตรีสวัสดิ์ลูกรัก พ่อรักลูกนะ" พ่อพูด จากนั้นเขาก็จูบที่หน้าผากของลูกชาย

"I will always love you. Goodnight!"
"พ่อรักลูกเสมอนะ ราตรีสวัสดิ์จ้ะ"

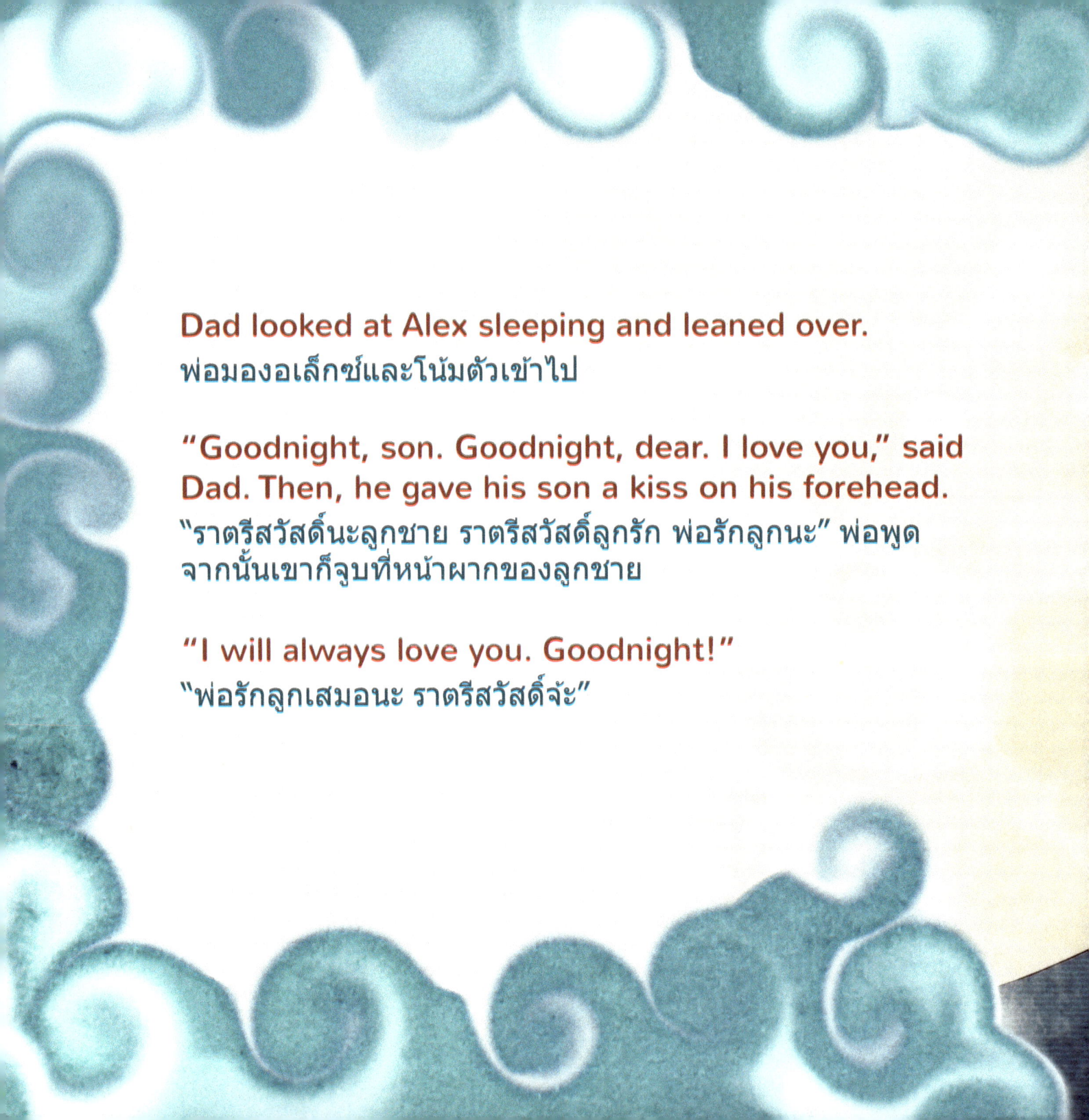

More GREAT children's books
พบกับหนังสือเด็กอีกมากมาย ได้ที่

www.kidkiddos.com

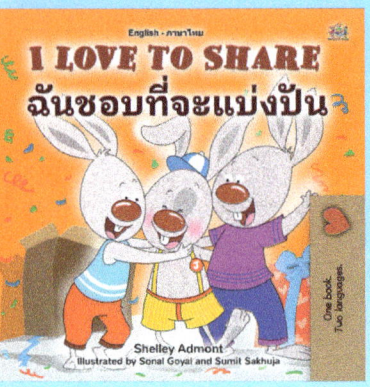

Scan the code to get a
FREE bilingual eBook

40 languages available

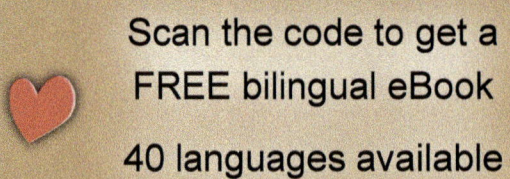

www.ingramcontent.com/pod-product-compliance
Lightning Source LLC
Chambersburg PA
CBHW061130070526
44584CB00033B/4280